Popular Classics

Wise Publications
London/New York/Paris/Sydney/
Copenhagen/Madrid

Exclusive Distributors:
Music Sales Limited
8/9 Frith Street, London W1V 5TZ, England.
Music Sales Pty Limited
120 Rothschild Avenue, Rosebery, NSW 2018, Australia.
Music Sales Corporation
257 Park Avenue South, New York, NY10010, United States of America.

Order No. AM952611
ISBN 0-7119-7267-2
This book © Copyright 1998 by Wise Publications

Music compiled and arranged by Stephen Duro
Music processed by Allegro Reproductions
Cover photograph courtesy of Digital Vision Ltd

Printed in the United Kingdom by
Halstan & Co Limited, Amersham, Buckinghamshire.

Your Guarantee of Quality

As publishers, we strive to produce every book to the highest commercial standards.

The music has been freshly engraved and the book has been carefully designed to minimise
awkward page turns and to make playing from it a real pleasure.

Particular care has been given to specifying acid-free, neutral-sized paper made from pulps
which have not been elemental chlorine bleached. This pulp is from farmed sustainable forests
and was produced with special regard for the environment.

Throughout, the printing and binding have been planned to ensure a sturdy, attractive publication
which should give years of enjoyment.

If your copy fails to meet our high standards, please inform us and we will gladly replace it.

Music Sales' complete catalogue describes thousands of titles and is available in full colour sections
by subject, direct from Music Sales Limited. Please state your areas of interest
and send a cheque/postal order for £1.50 for postage to:
Music Sales Limited, Newmarket Road, Bury St. Edmunds, Suffolk IP33 3YB.

Visit the Internet Music Shop at
http://www.musicsales.co.uk

Anvil Chorus
from Il Trovatore

Composed by Giuseppe Verdi

Majestic

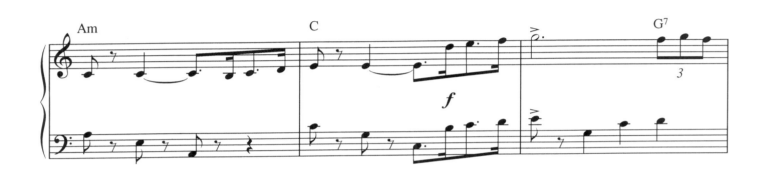

Aria

from Orfeo

Composed by C. W. von Gluck

Moderately slow

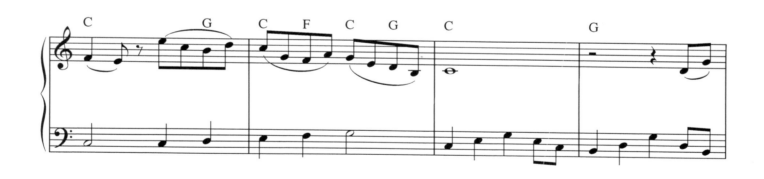

Ave Maria

Composed by Franz Schubert

Moderately slow

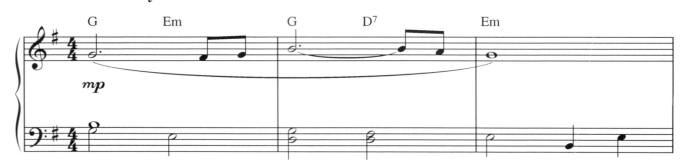

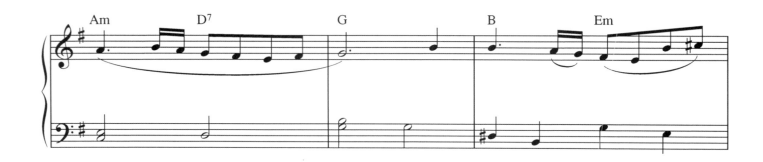

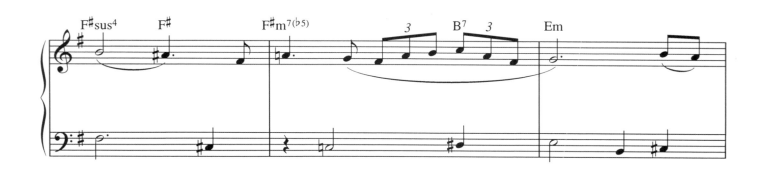

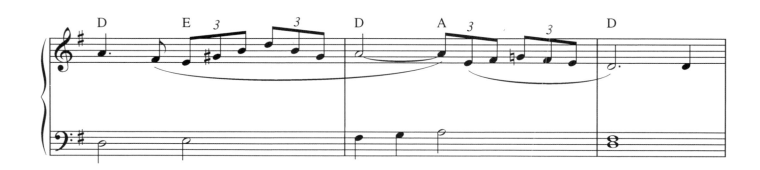

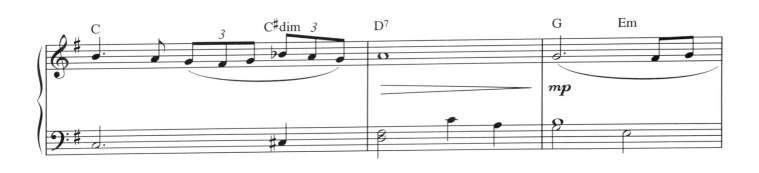

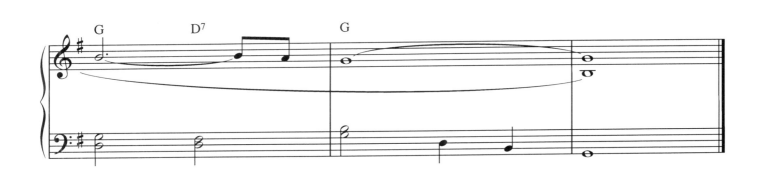

Chorus Of The Hebrew Slaves
from Nabucco

Composed by Giuseppe Verdi

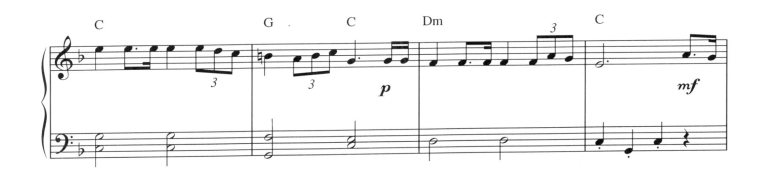

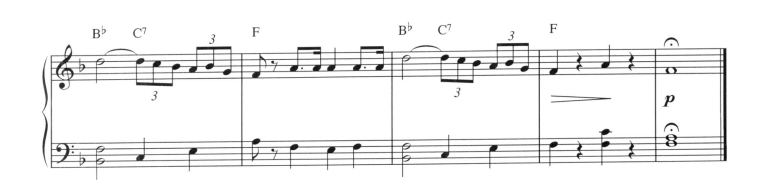

Clarinet Concerto
(Slow Movement Theme)

Composed by Wolfgang Amadeus Mozart

Dreaming

Composed by Robert Schumann

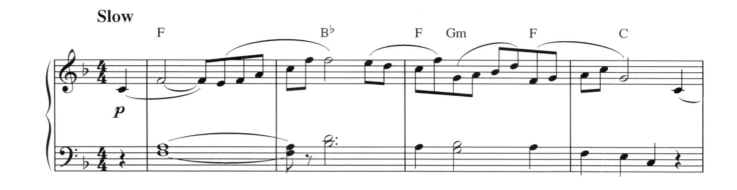

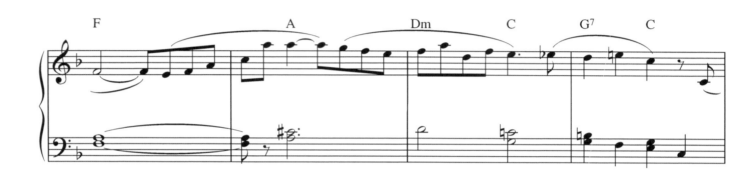

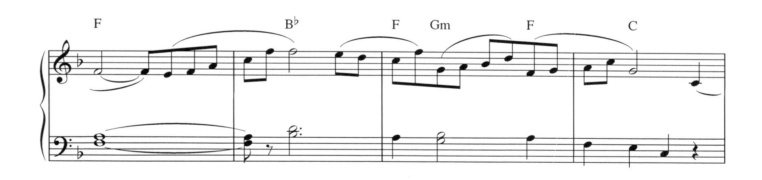

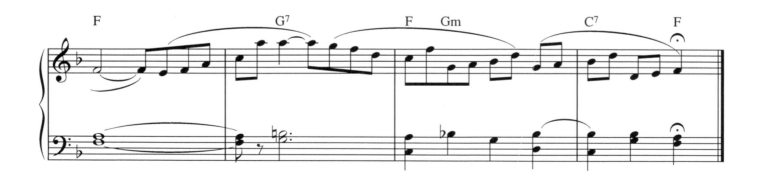

Jerusalem

Composed by Sir C. H. H. Parry

Moderately

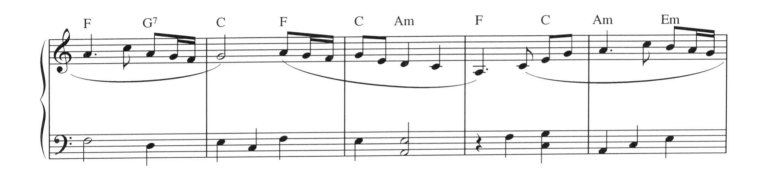

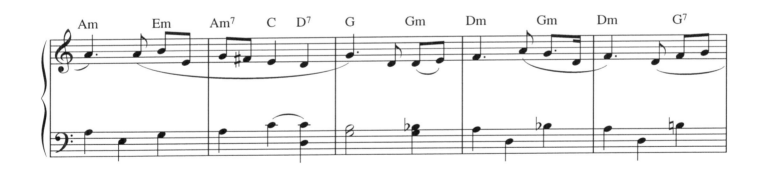

La Réjouissance
from the Fireworks Music

Composed by George Frideric Handel

Bright

Lullaby

Composed by Johannes Brahms

Marche Militaire

Composed by Franz Schubert

Moderately bright

March Of The Kings

from L'Arlésienne

Composed by Georges Bizet

Meditation
from Thais

Composed by Jules Massenet

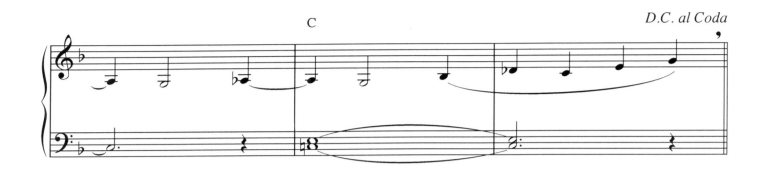

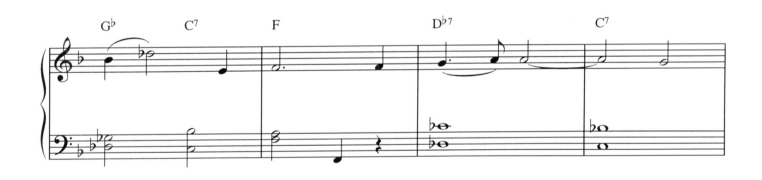

23

Pastoral Symphony
(Theme)

Composed by Ludwig van Beethoven

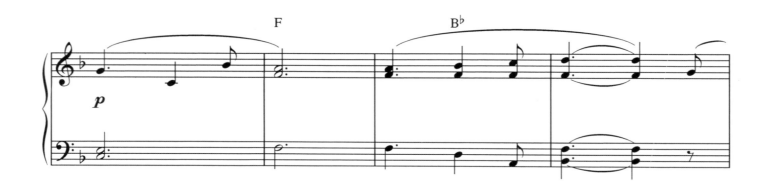

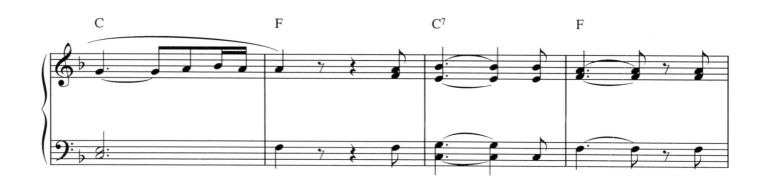

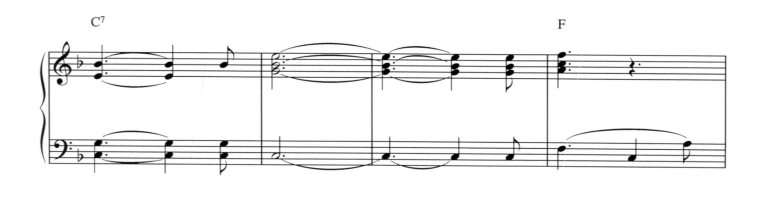

Panis Angelicus

Composed by César Franck

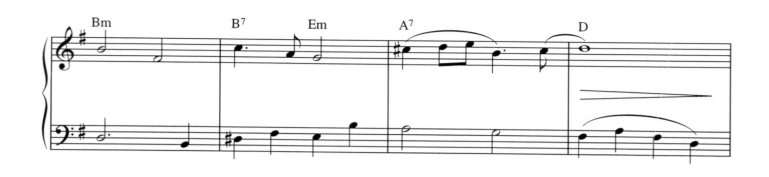

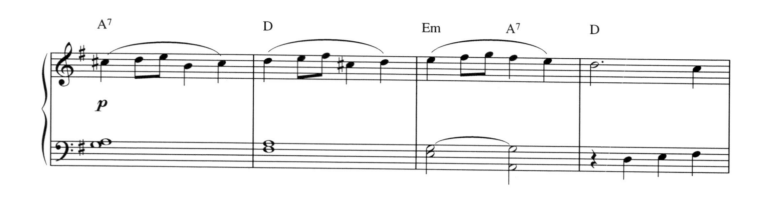

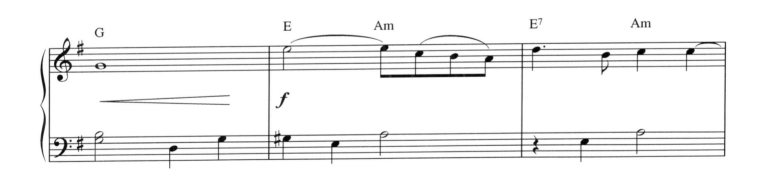

Prelude

from the Te Deum

Composed by Marc-Antoine Charpentier

Majestically

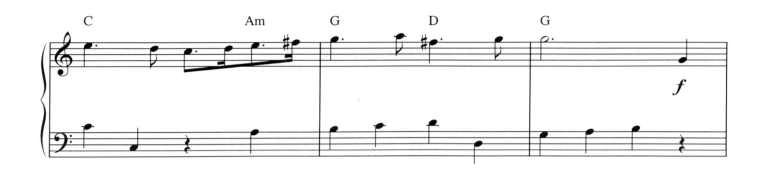

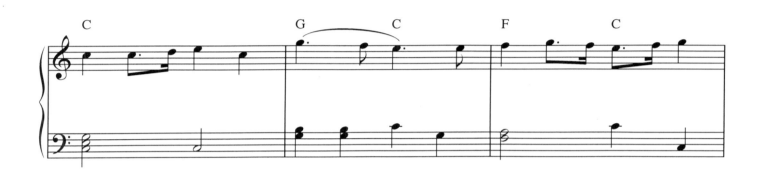

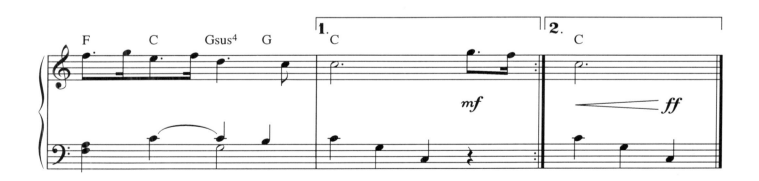

Romance
from Eine Kleine Nachtmusik

Composed by Wolfgang Amadeus Mozart

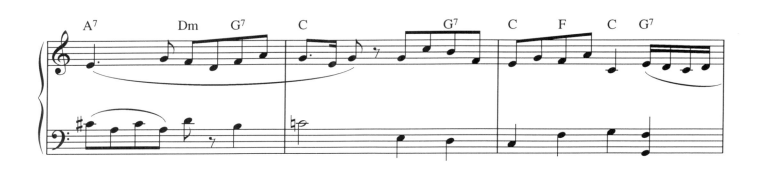

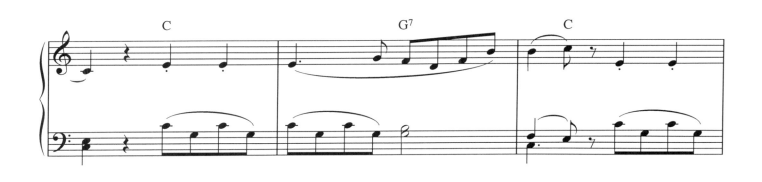

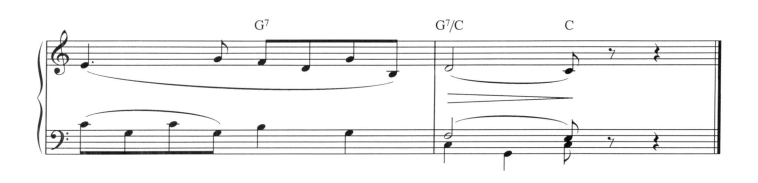

Roses From The South

Composed by Johann Strauss

a tempo

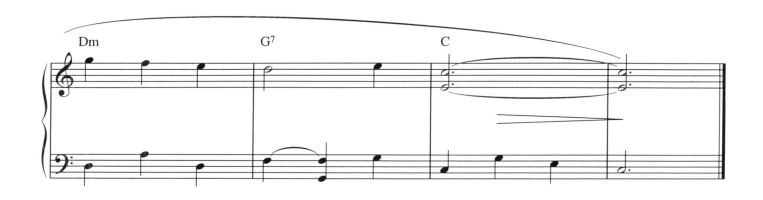

Skaters' Waltz

Composed by Emil Waldteufel

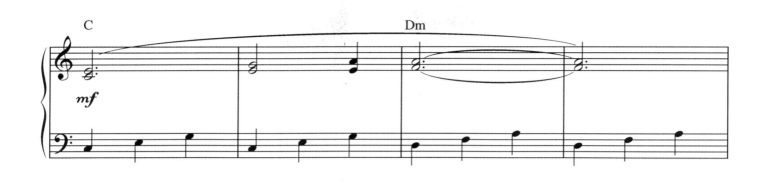

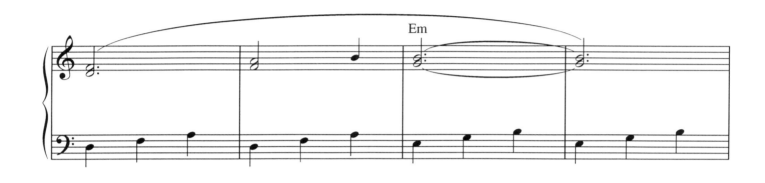

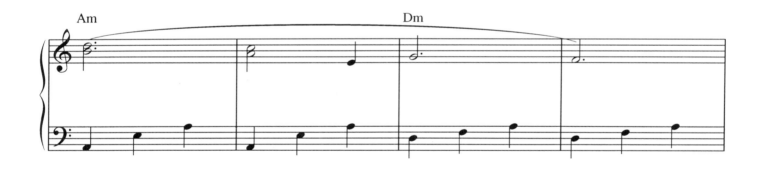

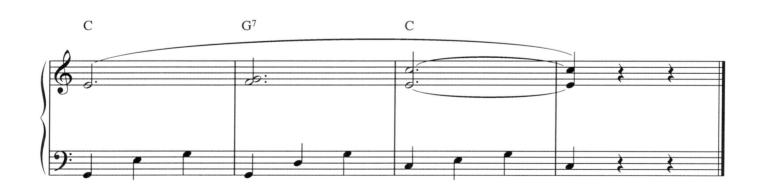

The Last Spring

Composed by Edvard Grieg

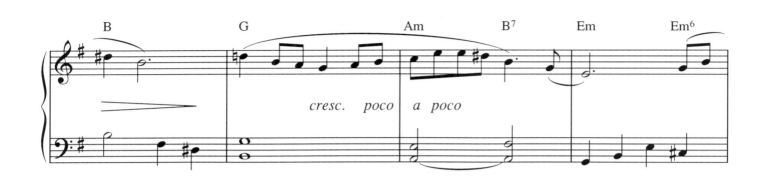

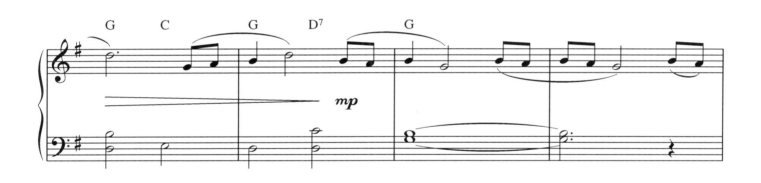

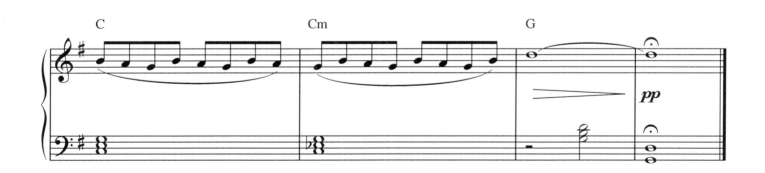

Toreador's Song

from Carmen

Composed by Georges Bizet

March tempo

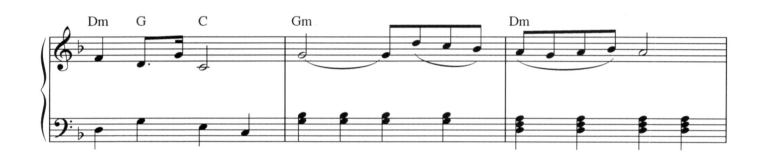

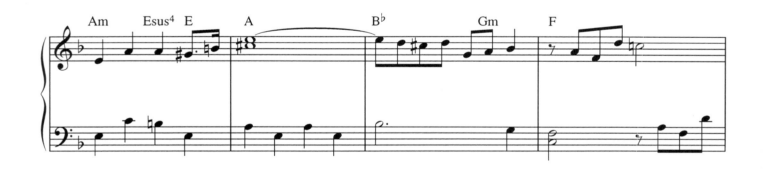

Waltz
from Coppelia

Composed by Léo Delibes

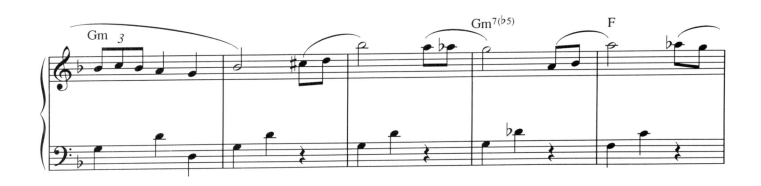

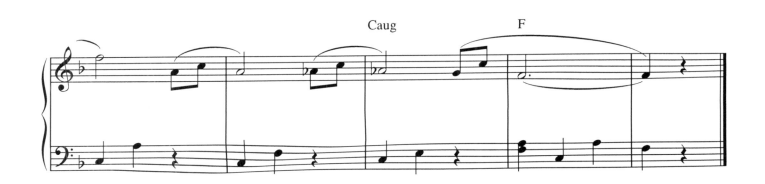

Waltz

from Swan Lake

Composed by Pyotr Ilyich Tchaikovsky

William Tell Overture

(Theme)

Composed by Gioacchino Rossini

Rondo
from Abdelazer
Composed by Henry Purcell